WHY READ CHURCH HISTORY?

J. Philip Arthur

*Now all these things happened, and they were
written for our admonition, upon whom
the ends of the ages have come.*

1 Corinthians 10:11

THE BANNER OF TRUTH TRUST

THE BANNER OF TRUTH TRUST

3 Murrayfield Road, Edinburgh EH12 6EL, UK
PO Box 621, Carlisle, PA 17013, USA

*

© The Banner of Truth Trust 2015

ISBN
Print: 978 1 84871 527 1
EPUB: 978 1 84871 528 8
Kindle: 978 1 84871 529 5

*

Typeset in 11/15 pt Adobe Garamond Pro at
The Banner of Truth Trust
Printed in the USA by
Versa Press, Inc.,
East Peoria, IL.

*

Scripture quotations are taken from the Holy Bible,
New King James Version, © Thomas Nelson, 1982.

WHY READ CHURCH HISTORY?

A lifelong passion

History has always been one of the great loves of my life. It is something I learned from my father while I was a very small boy. His passion to understand his own roots, and his conviction that the people of the past were worth getting to know, were infectious and communicated themselves to me in all sorts of ways. I grew up in the North East of England and my father was a coal miner. (Mining was the dominant industry in that part of the England at that time). I recall looking out over the North Sea as he asked me to imagine Viking long-ships approaching the shore, and in my mind I was transported twelve hundred years back in time. Occasions when we visited Northumbrian castles, tramped along sections of Hadrian's Wall, explored Durham Cathedral, and walked around the ancient heart of my home-town of Sunderland, have all left indelible memories. In addition, studying the Protestant Reformation of the sixteenth century at university marked a turning point in my Christian life. I admired the tough-minded, rational, disciplined piety of the reformers and saw in them a generation of Christian men who combined rugged courage with a profound conviction that an intellect that is not used to promote the glory of God is wasted.

I feel a real sense of loss when I meet people who have no time for the study of history. Do they know what they are missing? Perhaps it was spoiled for them during their school days. (Some teachers have a lot to answer for!) It troubles me even more when Christians, of all people, convince themselves that the past has nothing useful to say to the present. This attitude is often second cousin to what C. S. Lewis called 'chronological snobbery', the idea that the latest thing is always the best thing, the idea that technologically sophisticated twenty-first-century people have little to learn from the inhabitants of less-enlightened ages! Think like this and we run the risk of arrogance. Are modern Christians so successful that we cannot be taught by those who served God in earlier generations?

The Bible teaches a doctrine of history

The apostle Paul told the believers in Corinth to pay close attention to the various historical incidents recorded in the Old Testament. 'Now all these things happened to them as examples, and they were written for our admonition, upon whom the ends of the ages have come' (1 Cor. 10:11). Surely, if first-century Christians were to profit from the examples of those who served God in earlier generations, then so should we!

There is, however, an even more compelling reason for cultivating an appetite for the past. When the Hebrews were about to enter the promised land, Joshua ordered the construction of a pillar made from twelve stones, taken from the bed of the Jordan River, and he told the people, 'When your children ask their fathers in time to come, saying, "What are these stones?" then you shall let your children know, saying, "Israel crossed over this Jordan on dry land"; for the LORD your God dried up the waters of the Jordan before you until you had crossed over, as the LORD your God did to the Red Sea, which he dried up before us until we had crossed over, that all the peoples of the earth may know the hand of the LORD, that it is mighty, that you may fear the LORD your God forever' (Josh. 4:21b-24). Imagine the scene two or three generations down the road. Children playing by the river bank have noticed a strange column of stones, each one of them smooth, looking as though they had come from the bed of the river itself. So they ask their grandparents, too old now to be hard at work in the fields, 'What are these stones doing here?' The old folks reply, 'Well you see, not all that long ago, when my father was a boy, the Lord did something wonderful in the story of our nation. Let me tell you about it…'

In the same way, the mighty acts of God did not cease with Acts 28. If we close our minds to church history we say in effect that the story of what God has done since that time means nothing to us.

Nevertheless, we must proceed with caution. It is possible to learn the wrong lessons from the past.

Pitfalls to avoid

It is fatally easy to develop an *uncritical admiration for our heroes*, but no one is beyond criticism. One of the most refreshing things about the Bible is that it never conceals the faults of God's servants. There are numerous examples we could mention, of people who reached extraordinary levels of moral and spiritual eminence who nevertheless had a character flaw that was exposed. For example, our admiration for all that King David achieved is tempered by our knowledge of his adultery with Bathsheba. Similarly, despite the apostle Peter's importance in the early days of the Christian church no attempt is made to cover up his betrayal of Jesus. The sheer honesty of the way the Bible handles the lives of its great men and women in general is all the more important when we encounter the Lord Jesus Christ, the one figure who is portrayed with a *flawless* character.

With the example of Scripture before us, our assessment of the great Christians of the past must be sane. Some evangelical biographies come perilously close to hagiography and are as uncritical and adulatory as some lives of the saints written in Medieval times. Yet even the best of men are only men at best, and we do well to remember it. Even as we challenge our own hearts to imitate the consecration, dogged courage, and unremitting labours of the saints of long ago, we must be mentally ready to recognise their mistakes and resolve to avoid them.

For the same reason, the doctrinal legacy of an earlier generation of Christian teachers should never be swallowed whole. Our admiration for Luther's recovery of the doctrine of justification by faith alone should not blind us to the fact that the great German reformer could not abandon the idea that the body of Christ was, in some sense, physically present in the bread eaten at the Lord's Table.

Many of us are grateful for Augustine's contribution to succeeding generations of Christian teachers. The story of the way this tormented and wayward genius came to faith in Christ in a garden in Milan is fascinating. As a young man, he had thrown himself into a life of pleasure. He had crossed every boundary in his quest for fulfilment. He had even flirted for a time with an extreme religious cult. Now, approaching middle age, he was desperate. For all that he was one of the foremost academics of the age, satisfaction eluded him and he could not control destructive habits learned in his teens. Drifting over the garden wall, he heard the voice of a child: 'Pick it up and read it, pick it up and read it …' On the ground before him, lay the Epistle to the Romans. He opened it at 13:13-14. In a moment, his world was turned upside-down and his massive intellect was recruited for the Christian cause. The story of his conversion was recounted in his *Confessions* which were written between 397 and 398 A.D., perhaps the first Christian autobiography ever written. Many modern believers are also very appreciative of the doughty stand that Augustine took against the British monk Pelagius, when he defended the Bible's teaching on the sovereignty of God and free grace. But at the same time, we would do well to bear in mind that his arguments in favour of compelling the Donatists[1] to conform gave some credibility to later Roman Catholic arguments in favour of persecuting heretics, including Protestants.

Surely the vital thing is to cultivate the Berean spirit (Acts 17:11), a readiness to give a patient hearing to the teachers of the past, but to scrutinise all that they said in the light of God's word. In other words, we apply to the teachers of the past the same test that we would use for the teachers we admire today. Only Scripture is infallible.

[1] Donatism was a movement that grew up in North Africa in the 4th century, mainly among Berber people, as a response to the persecution of Christians mounted by the Emperor Diocletian. Once the period of persecution died down, one of the most difficult and divisive issues that divided Christians was the treatment of those believers who had given way under persecution and now expressed remorse and wished to be received back into communion. Some were even clergy. The Donatists tended to take a more rigorous line on the issue than others.

Incidentally, it is possible to err in the opposite direction, to conclude that the sins and failings of yesterday's spiritual giants mean that they not only have feet of clay but are made of nothing but clay from head to toe. Perhaps in some respects we see further than they do, but a pygmy sitting on the shoulders of a giant may well see a little more clearly than the colossus who supports him. Even so, we all know which is the giant and which the pygmy. A rapid writer, working at ten hours a day, would need a lifetime to transcribe what Martin Luther wrote in twenty-five years. Fifty-five volumes, by no means his total output, have been translated into English. When we who have achieved so little venture to criticise men who have dared and achieved so much, we do well to couch our censures in modest language.

It has to be said that some like to escape into the past because they find it more attractive and congenial than the present. For people of a certain temperament, historical study can become a way of evading our duty to our own generation. Spend too much time reflecting on the way that Whitefield spread the gospel and you may never get round to spreading it yourself. A rigorous critique of the evangelists of a bygone era certainly has its value, but if the dead could speak, would they not challenge our generation as follows, 'I prefer the way that I did it to the way that you don't do it'?

We also need to be alive to the danger of assuming that because God worked in certain ways in the past, we can reproduce the results by copying the approach right down to matters of detail. Jonathan Edwards was a remarkably gifted theologian and philosopher who was active in New England in the decades just prior to American independence. When he preached his great sermon, 'Sinners in the Hands of an Angry God', first to his own congregation in Northampton, Massachusetts, and then in Enfield, Connecticut, on 8 July 1741, the results were astounding.[2] We cannot guarantee similar results by reading the same sermon any more than we could expect a second Pentecost if we read Acts 2 in the presence of 3,000 people. Lawyers may be bound by precedent, God is not. The past teaches us that great things can be achieved when God sees fit to honour preaching and prayer. It is unwise to press the point further than that.

It is also wise to recognise that we could not transplant men and women who served God well in a very different time and culture into the world that we know today. We do not need eighteenth-century Christians today, but modern Christians of eighteenth-century calibre. In the same way, we do not need, and therefore should not pray for, another Spurgeon. We must ask the Lord for gifted and consecrated preachers who will speak to our own time with the same fervour and effectiveness that Spurgeon spoke to Victorian London.

There is also the equal and opposite error to avoid, namely the tendency to look at the men and movements of the past through modern spectacles. It is all too easy to look at some of the protest movements of the Middle Ages and read our own kind of church life back into them. Are we too sensitive to Rome's claim that the apostolic succession of the pope and the bishops gives her unbroken institutional continuity with the past? Is it really necessary to try to create an apostolic succession of our own? For instance, it does

[2] It is worth noting that Edwards' approach would probably not commend him to a tutor in homiletics at a Bible seminary. The sermon had ten headings. Edwards usually preached in a quiet voice, with his notes held close to his face (he was short-sighted). Authority and unction are not dependent on volume.

not necessarily follow that because certain movements were persecuted by the Church of Rome that they were therefore orthodox forerunners of the evangelical churches of today.

Finally, there is a danger of concentrating so much on the people, movements, and events themselves that we fail to see the hand of God at work. The biblical historian who penned Psalm 44 could never be accused of that: 'For they did not get possession of the land by their own sword, nor did their own arm save them, but it was your right hand, your arm, and the light of your countenance, because you favoured them.' (Psa. 44:3). The great deeds of Luther, Whitefield, or Spurgeon aren't worth studying if we forget to identify the mighty acts of Christ through these men! When I was cutting my teeth as an inexperienced preacher, I was given superb advice from one of my mentors, Rev. Tom Johnson of Hartlepool: 'Remember to put the crown on the right head.' We can do nothing better as we look into the story of the church. The most compelling reason to pick up a Christian biography is to marvel at what God has done.

Tracing the footsteps of God

Henry Ford is chiefly famed for his part in founding the motor company that still bears his name. He is also famous for an off-the-cuff remark to the effect that 'history is bunk'. Sometimes I come across evangelical Christians who are almost as dismissive about the value of learning from the past, an attitude that says, 'That was then; this is now.' I prefer the perspective of an early Puritan historian of the first colonists in New England, who termed his work *The Mighty Acts of Christ in America*. Is there anything to be learned from what God has done? How can any thoughtful believer respond to that question with a negative answer?

First of all, we will learn a measure of respect for the achievements of our spiritual ancestors and a degree of humility about our own. Compared with ourselves, they achieved so much with so little. When, after a year spent in the Wartburg Castle from 1521 to 1522, Martin Luther produced his translation of the New Testament in German he was not able to call on the enormous battery of linguistic tools available to the modern translator.[3] William Tyndale, the first man to translate the New Testament into English out of the original Greek, did so as a hunted fugitive. Not for him the calm seclusion of a well-equipped library. He produced a literary and spiritual masterpiece while on the run from men who wanted him dead. This ought also to give us a new admiration for the theological achievements of the reformers and Puritans. Facilities that academics in the West now take for granted were denied these men, but who could read a page or two from Calvin's *Institutes*[4] or one of his commentaries, without recognising that here was a man with a rare depth of insight into the word of God.

History also teaches us that error is not original. The truths of Christianity can only be attacked at certain key points. Heresy

[3] A complete German Bible, including the Old Testament was published in 1534. This was the work of a team of scholars including Luther and a number of his associates, notably Philip Melanchthon but also several others.

[4] John Calvin produced his first Latin edition of *Institutes of the Christian Religion* in 1536. It was intended to be a wide-ranging handbook to the Christian faith for those who already had some introductory knowledge. The fifth, definitive, Latin edition, produced in 1559, was five times as large as the first. Calvin also translated the Latin editions into French and in doing so did much to aid the consolidation of metropolitan French. A new very readable English translation of Calvin's 1541 edition of the *Institutes* is available from the Banner of Truth Trust.

is predictable. Some movements that we encounter today are recycled versions of others that existed centuries ago. Roman Catholicism is a highly developed and very elaborate form of the Galatian heresy (Christ plus works and ceremonies) which the apostle Paul confounded in the first century. This can save us a great deal of hard work. When we come across a new cult, we will often find that the answer to it has already been worked out when an earlier generation of the Lord's people met something similar to it. There is no need to reinvent the wheel! New Age critiques of Christianity (one of the most recent is Dan Brown's blockbuster novel, *The Da Vinci Code*) are actually covering very old ground indeed, doing little more than repeat the worn-out arguments advanced by the Gnostics in the second century A.D. In the same way, since the Arian heresy was successfully combated by Athanasius in the fourth century A.D., there is no real need for us to work out a defence against those modern Arians, the Jehovah's Witnesses, from first principles.

Another advantage is that history gives us long perspectives. It can be all too easy to assume that evangelical normality is represented by the Christian scene that we ourselves have known and what we have learned from the generation immediately before us (and in some cases reacted against). During my lifetime, evangelical Christianity in Britain has been dominated by two influences. Both have been extremely pervasive. The first was the high-profile campaign evangelism that made its way to the UK from North America in the second half of the nineteenth century. The second has been the Charismatic movement. The earlier Pentecostal movement came to Britain as recently as 1905, the newer Charismatic development of it came during my boyhood in the 1960s. How easy it would be for anyone born in the present century to assume that what they knew from their own experience was the norm. Speaking personally, when I first came under pressure from Charismatics who wanted me to believe that the way to spiritual power was to buy into their package of second-blessing theology and the resultant gifts, I was able to use the past to throw light on the present. Men of God like Whitefield and Spurgeon lived out their days before these emphases became fashionable, yet knew far more of the power of God on their ministries than most moderns.

A journey through the past can also teach us a valuable lesson in tolerance. How large are our sympathies? Adoniram Judson and his first wife Ann were among the first group of American missionaries to leave the United States for the purposes of cross-cultural mission. Congregationalists may not like the fact that Adoniram Judson became a Baptist on his way to serve the Lord in Burma. They nevertheless have to admit that it did not mean the end of him as a useful servant of the gospel! Baptists like myself also have to acknowledge that until the nineteenth century, the overwhelming bulk of the eminent saints of God whose names are revered and whose stories are still told, practised the sprinkling of infants. God used them for all that! A good test for a British Calvinist is whether he has a place in his heart for that consecrated and zealous Arminian John Wesley. Should we of all people be surprised at this? We cherish the doctrines of God's sovereignty. Is a sovereign Lord not free to bless whomsoever he pleases? And if we cannot learn anything about the atonement from a John Wesley, he may have a thing or two to teach us about fervour and love for Christ. Historians two centuries from now may even be extolling the Christlikeness of certain late twentieth-century Charismatics!

For a British Christian, one especially poignant dimension to all this is that much of the story of the work of God in the British Isles tells a sad story. How low we have sunk! We are not worthy of our fathers. We find ourselves echoing the words of the Psalmist, 'We have heard with our ears, O God, our fathers have told us, what work you did in their days, in the times of old.' (Psa. 44:1). One conference, held each year, attracts about three hundred Reformed ministers. In the year 1662, 2,000 ministers refused to compromise on a point of principle and were ejected from the national church. Given that the population of England was much smaller then, an equivalent number today would be something in the region of 30,000. The tone of moral and spiritual life in our country would be vastly different if there were as many servants of the gospel willing to pay a high price for their obedience to Christ in our generation. And yet, in its way, this perspective is healthy. Only a few years ago, during the height of the agitation surrounding the 'Toronto Blessing', some Charismatics urged us to believe that we were living through a period of revival. It is only fair to observe that other Charismatic leaders would have shared the concerns of many that such triumphalism was sadly misplaced. Facing the fact that our country lies in a deep spiritual trough may not be comfortable, but surely realism will help our prayers to be all the more urgent.

Feeling at home in a strange land

The opening line of L. P. Hartley's novel *The Go-Between* reads, 'The past is a foreign country. They do things differently there.'

This phrase has become almost proverbial. When we try to understand the past, our first impression is often astonishment at the sheer strangeness of it all. Different clothes, different manners and social customs, and different notions about what constitutes the good life can often make the time-traveller from the twenty-first century feel distinctly odd.[5] Even so, we do have one point of contact with believers from previous ages that outweighs all the sense of strangeness that we encounter when we try to step back into a world that is no more. *They were Christians*. For all that unfamiliar surroundings can be taxing, one thing makes us feel at home. We are among people whose heart concerns are the same. Even if you feel that the Protestant reformers of Northern Europe lived half a world and four centuries away and are not your sort of person, can you not warm to them as men who had the same experience of saving grace that is so precious to you, men who loved the Jesus that you love and who wanted to serve him at least as earnestly as you do? Look at them in this way and you might even feel that they have something to offer as experienced older brothers!

Certainly in the modern West, the prevailing spiritual culture is superficial. For myself, I have always turned with some relief to the reformers and the Puritans because they valued a tough-minded, rational, disciplined piety that is light years away from the slipshod ethos of contemporary evangelicalism.

---

[5] The British historian Ian Mortimer has written two popular books which highlight this sense of difference between 'now' and 'then' called *The Time-Traveller's Guide to Medieval England* and *The Time-Traveller's Guide to Elizabethan England*.

Walking with giants

I feel sorry for the person who cannot be motivated by the stories of some of the great saints of an earlier period. Does your pulse not quicken as you think of William Carey who went to India in 1792 and had no fellowship with a Christian of his own race apart from his wife for six years? He never went back to England, spending forty-two years without a break in India. During that time he translated parts of the Bible into thirty-six languages, including six whole Bibles. When asked to explain the secret of his immense labours he replied, 'I can plod!'

I have not met many heroes in the flesh, but I have in the books I have read. It has done my soul good to stand alongside Luther as he defied the Emperor of Germany, to pray alongside warm-hearted Samuel Rutherford, and to go, at least in spirit, to Spurgeon's congregation in the Metropolitan Tabernacle. What a spur to wholehearted, no-compromise Christianity these men can be.

In the same way, you will never meet John Newton, converted slave-trader and author of the hymn 'Amazing Grace', in this life, but read a good biography of him and you will be amazed at what God can do in the life of just one man. Why not take a walk in the company of giants? If you then go on to read some of Newton's works,[6] you will find yourself getting closer to the heartbeat of the man himself and you will begin to enjoy fellowship with a Christian who has been in glory for two centuries.

Church history can be thrilling, especially when our own experience is very much an uphill struggle. How good to remind

[6] A new 4-volume edition of *The Works of John Newton* is now available from the Banner of Truth Trust. See 'Further Reading' for details.

ourselves what God can do, whether in the life of a single person or in a short period of time. The story of Christianity is packed with examples of situations which appeared to be at their lowest ebb, while out of sight God was preparing a man or group of men who would turn everything round in a matter of a few years. No situation is so bleak that God cannot overturn it!

Getting started in church history

I cannot think of a single Christian who would not benefit from acquiring a working knowledge of church history.

First and foremost, God has been at work in this world of ours ever since the events recorded in the final chapter of Acts 28. Time is always well spent if we spend it making a serious attempt to acquaint ourselves with some of the great things that God has done.

Secondly, we are not the first generation of Christians and we have much to learn, both positively and negatively, from the examples of fellow believers. There are stirring examples of men and women who served God in their generation with courage and persistence, whose stories will warm the heart and quicken the pulse of any serious Christian. It also has to be said that there are glaring examples of the damage that can be done when good men embrace errors or fall into sin.

Thirdly, the modern Christian scene is complex and it can be enormously helpful to have some understanding of the reasons why the evangelical world has developed the way it has.

But where should we begin? For a start, the task can seem very daunting. There is just so much of it. Academic historians usually specialise. It is not unusual to hear them excuse their ignorance about one particular area of history by saying, 'Not my period!' For those believers therefore, who feel overwhelmed at the thought of trying to master a grasp of all that God has done in twenty centuries, I would recommend a twin-track approach. The first track is to obtain a good general history, and the second is to get hold of some useful and stimulating biographies.

General history

The value of a general history is that it gives a broad brush treatment and will introduce the reader to the big issues in a way that combines the benefits of being comprehensive on the one hand and compact on the other. Two examples of this type are worth noting. The first is *Sketches from Church History* by S. M. Houghton,[7] which is an excellent appetiser in the sense that it gives a brief introduction to many thrilling episodes of God's dealings with his people down the years but leaves the reader wanting more. The second is a series of three volumes called *Two Thousand Years of Christ's Power* by Nick Needham. Dr Needham originally intended to produce four volumes in all, but as the series has grown it has become likely that at least five volumes will be necessary. It follows that this series is somewhat more thorough than S. M. Houghton's book but it has been deliberately written with the non-specialist in mind and so far, the author has succeeded in producing a marvel of condensation in a readable and entertaining style. The first volume covers the age of the early church fathers and introduces the reader to the characters and controversies of that era. Volume Two examines

[7] S. M. Houghton, *Sketches from Church History*, (Edinburgh: Banner of Truth Trust, 1980, repr. 2011).

the Middle Ages and does much to correct the view which many evangelicals have absorbed, that this was essentially a sterile period in the story of the church. Volume Three is a helpful survey of the Protestant Reformation. This was the period that I studied while a student at Cambridge, and I am often sorry that modern evangelicals have only a dim grasp of the issues at stake during the great spiritual conflicts of sixteenth century. This book will help Christians acquire a working knowledge of this important era that did so much to shape the modern world. Volume Four, on the seventeenth century, is due to be published in the near future.

Good biographies have their own fascination too. We often find it easier to identify with an individual than with a movement. The struggles and triumphs of a single fellow Christian can speak to the heart in a special way. The list of available material is big and growing. Evangelical Press for instance, have published works by authors such as Brian Edwards, Jim Cromarty, Faith Cook and Tim Shenton. I would like to pick out three works in particular.

The first is *God's Outlaw* by Brian Edwards.[8] This is an outstanding example of what might be termed an 'entry level' biography. It introduces the reader to the story of William Tyndale, a Gloucestershire man who died as a martyr in 1536, having become an exile from his native land because he was consumed with longing to provide his fellow countrymen with an accurate translation of the word of God. Edwards has caught the atmosphere of early Tudor England superbly and in a single volume, available at a modest price, the modern reader can be amazed at what God achieved through the life of a lonely scholar, and also be left in no doubt as to why the Reformation was necessary.

---

[8] Brian H. Edwards, *God's Outlaw* (Welwyn: Evangelical Press, 1976).

Edwards has made the sixteenth century come alive in this book and has also gone a long way to help us understand why that century in particular is so relevant to modern evangelicals.

My second choice is a more substantial piece of work, two hefty volumes by Arnold Dallimore on the life of George Whitefield, the eighteenth-century evangelist.[9] Some might be put off these books for no other reason than their sheer size, but I promise you, I found each of them a real page-turner and could not get through them quickly enough as I thrilled to learn the way that God was at work during the Evangelical Awakening that took place in Britain and North America during the middle decades of the eighteenth century. A big book is read page by page, chapter by chapter just as a small one is, and it is no chore to take on a substantial volume when every page unearths new triumphs of the gospel or new lessons for the church today.

In the same way, I would also heartily recommend Iain Murray's two-volume biography of Dr Martyn Lloyd-Jones.[10] Iain Murray has written several other historical studies, including a delightful life of Jonathan Edwards, but I appreciate his life of Lloyd-Jones especially because it is more than just a fascinating life of one of the most remarkable figures in twentieth-century Britain; it is also a most helpful survey of the whole evangelical scene as it developed in Britain before and after the Second World

[9] Arnold Dallimore, *George Whitefield: The Life and Times of the Great Evangelist of the Eighteenth-Century Revival*, 2 vols. (Edinburgh: Banner of Truth Trust, 1970 [vol. 1], 1980 [vol. 2]).

[10] Iain H. Murray, *David Martyn Lloyd-Jones: The First Forty Years, 1899–1939*, (Edinburgh: Banner of Truth Trust, 1982) & *David Martyn Lloyd-Jones: The Fight of Faith, 1939–1981* (Edinburgh: Banner of Truth Trust, 1990). A new one-volume abridged edition (with some new material) entitled *The Life of Martyn Lloyd-Jones, 1899–1981*, was published by the Trust in 2013.

War. This book helped me understand the evangelical world that I knew when I first became a Christian.

Before I close, I ought to mention two other sets of books that will help Christians, particularly in Great Britain, to appreciate their heritage, and which will also be a real help to any believer who feels that even a modest sized book may be too much to take on.

Firstly there is the series of Travel Guides produced by Day One. These small volumes are in a soft-back format that can fit happily into a pocket or handbag. They combine a brief but stimulating biography with a guide to places where there is still some association with the person concerned. With their help you can discover where John Knox is buried, where Spurgeon was baptised, and where Thomas Cranmer was burned at the stake. Like any series, this one is a little patchy and while all are worth having, the volumes on Spurgeon, Lloyd-Jones, J. C. Ryle, and the martyrs who died during the reign of Mary Tudor are particular highlights.

Secondly, Evangelical Press have recently published a series of 'Bite-size biographies', attractively priced and modest sized books, which should not be intimidating to anyone.

FURTHER READING

Unless otherwise stated, published by the Banner of Truth Trust

General History

S. M. Houghton, *Sketches from Church History*
N. Needham, *Two Thousand Years of Christ's Power,* (Grace Publications)

   Vol. 1: *The Early Church Fathers*

   Vol. 2: *The Middle Ages*

   Vol. 3: *The Renaissance and Reformation*

   Vol. 4: *The Seventeenth Century* (publication anticipated in the near future)

Christian Biography

Brian Edwards, *God's Outlaw* (EP)
Iain H. Murray, *D. Martyn Lloyd-Jones*

   Vol. 1: *The First Forty Years 1899–1939*

   Vol. 2: *The Fight of Faith 1939–1981*

Josiah Bull, *The Life of John Newton*
Andrew Bonar, *Robert Murray M'Cheyne*
Arnold Dallimore, *George Whitefield*, Vol. 1
Arnold Dallimore, *George Whitefield*, Vol. 2
Arnold Dallimore, *Spurgeon A New Biography*
W. J. Grier, *The Life of John Calvin*
Bitesize Biographies (EP)
Travel With Series (DayOne)

Iain H. Murray

> *Amy Carmichael: 'Beauty for Ashes', A Biography*
> *Archibald G. Brown: Spurgeon's Successor*

Paul E. Brown, *Ernest Kevan, Leader in Twentieth Century British Evangelicalism*

Faith Cook,

> *Selina, Countess of Huntingdon*
> *Samuel Rutherford and His Friends*
> *Sound of Trumpets*
> *Singing in the Fire*
> *William Grimshaw of Haworth*

J. C. Ryle, *Five English Reformers*

Douglas Higgins, *Autobiography of a Yorkshire Christian*

Five Pioneer Missionaries

Bethan Lloyd-Jones, *Memories of Sandfields*

William Blair & Bruce Hunt, *The Korean Pentecost and the Sufferings which Followed*

John Weir, *The Ulster Awakening: An Account of the 1859 Revival in Ireland*

Christian Doctrine

John Calvin, *Institutes of the Christian Religion, 1541 edition*